T0102974

Leadership, Eh?

How to Lead, Laugh & Win in the Game of Business & Life

by
Murray R. Janewski

Order this book online at www.trafford.com
or email orders@trafford.com

Most Trafford titles are also available at major online book retailers.

Print information available on the last page.

ISBN: 978-1-4251-8739-2 (sc)
ISBN: 978-1-4269-4020-0 (e)

Trafford rev. 07/22/2015

Trafford PUBLISHING www.trafford.com
North America & international
toll-free: 1 888 232 4444 (USA & Canada)
fax: 812 355 4082

Contents

Introduction and Dedication

SO YOU THINK you're a leader, eh? Well, then, you need to meet Ernie. My dad introduced him to me many years ago, while he was writing his book, *The Travels of Ernie*. I learned that Ernie had been many places and seen many things, and I soon realized that the advice being given by this fictitious character was really my dad's.

I began learning about leadership at a very young age. When I played hockey as a kid, my father would remind me once in a while to "be a leader out there." It was years later before I finally realized that he wasn't preparing me for the game, he was preparing me for life.

With my father's blessing, I decided to promote Ernie to be my boss, my leader, and my mentor, and to start sharing the valuable leadership lessons that I have learned from many people, in many places. My dad encouraged me to start writing any leadership stories I could, whether from my own experiences, or from stories that others had passed on to me. He said, "You worry about the leadership stuff and I can help you with the Ernie stuff (the wit and humor)." I wrote the first two stories that you see in this book and e-mailed them to my dad for his critical review. His e-mail reply came back a few days later: "You don't need my help." That in itself was the leadership and inspiration I needed to keep writing.

Ernie is a witty, lovable character who has incredible wisdom. You can enjoy the stories one at a time, starting anyplace in the book that grabs your attention. I've had a ball meeting people and documenting the stories they have shared with me, and being able to tell them through Ernie.

Although he was not alive while I collected and wrote the other sixteen stories, my dad was certainly a part of it. I therefore dedicate this book in honor of the greatest leader I have known—my father, Bill Janewski.

1

Leadership—What is it?

I STUMBLED INTO Ernie's truck to head out for a day visiting some of our facilities in the field. It was early morning, and I had been up late the night before watching a hockey frenzy, as two teams battled for the Stanley Cup in a seventh and deciding game. A little groggy from the festivities that go along with this type of "entertainment," I was bemused by how many times I'd heard the media talk about leadership in competitive sports. You know, all they can say is the winning team "dug deep" and, "with strong leadership," they got it done. You would think the media would try to explain why it's always leadership that wins the game, and it amazes me that they don't.

So I thought I would ask Ernie—he would surely be able to explain the essence of why leadership is so important. I waited for him to swallow a big gulp of coffee, clear his throat, and—as usual—complain about the "double-double" being too sweet.

"Ernie," I started, "why does the media always peg competitive success to leadership, without ever really explaining it?"

After a moment of silence he started the truck, pulled out, and said, "I've been many places and seen many things." (I knew this to be a truism.) "Firstly, the media doesn't have to explain anything." (This was now also a truism.) But secondly, and more pertinent to your question, leadership is *not* important."

"How could that be?" I asked. Maybe I was asking the wrong guy here.

"What's important is how you feel when you're being led," Ernie stated in a matter-of-fact way.

I waited for his next swallow of coffee and more grumbling. I knew now was not the time to prompt him, as this might interrupt his thoughts and prevent something profound—which was what I was after. And I wasn't disappointed.

"Can you remember a time when you were truly inspired by someone?" asked Ernie.

"Many times," I replied.

After more silence, I knew he was waiting for me to expound. Again, I did not want to discourage his "Sermon on the Mount," so I thought of a time about fifteen years ago.

"I once traveled to the other side of the country," I began. I thought this might impress such a well-traveled man. "In fact, I settled for three years in a small city. I met a guy named Mick, and after getting to know him and his love for music, we started jamming now and then. He really inspired me to learn about blues music."

"Wonderful," said Ernie, himself an accomplished musician. "You can learn a lot through music. Tell me, did you feel compelled to say 'thanks, boss' to this Mick fellow?"

"Actually, I met him through work and I was *his* boss," I said, beginning to smile as I sensed where Ernie was going.

"So leadership becomes a situational thing… say, do you think Mick could lead a whole group of musicians who really wanted to play?" asked Ernie, suddenly coming to life.

"Why, you thinking of forming a blues band?" I chortled as I watched him spit out the window. Actually, that might have been a prerequisite to being in a blues band—the spitting, that is. Anyway, Ernie never answered my question. Instead he asked me, "What if some guys in the group were more accomplished than others—would he treat them all the same?"

I reflected on a few jam sessions where others were involved, and immediately I knew the answer. "Heck, no," I said. "I'd experienced endless instruction and coaching from Mick, in between jam sessions, just to be able to get a single lick in one song. With another guy, he just had to nod his head and this fellow took off on a perfect lead interval. And another time we stopped and Mick suggested we make a few changes to one part of a song. Then off we went—all really enjoying it."

"Then I would profess," announced Ernie, "that your friend Mick is somewhat of a natural leader in what he has a passion for. He shares that passion with the whole group. Everyone steps up a notch, creating better results and enjoying it at the same time."

"You bet!" I exclaimed.

"So keep in mind that leadership itself is not important. *What you do with it to influence others* is important. And you need to look at each individual in each situation to know how to influence them, or to help them reach higher levels of performance."

I sat quietly, reflecting on everything Ernie had just said. It seemed like common sense to me, yet Ernie had a way of really helping me understand. It had been that way for years. By his own definition, then, Ernie was a true leader. I thought I should let him know that.

Just before stopping for another coffee I said, "Ernie, you know that I've always considered you a true leader."

"Thanks," he said.

"But now I realize that it's not important," I said, thinking myself quite cunning.

Ernie rolled back his eyes as he ordered another "double-double."

2

Self-Deceit

ONE MORNING, WHILE I was shaving, I was thinking about leadership and how critical it is for success, not only in business, but in all aspects of life: as a parent, as a friend, in sports, and in the community. I was troubled by where to start in order to become a better leader.

It was a bright and sunny Saturday, so I made my way over to Ernie's. He had the coffee on, so I invited myself in.

"You can just walk in whenever you want," announced Ernie.

"I just did," I replied.

"I hadn't noticed," Ernie said, "but you won't like the coffee—it's pretty strong for a young man like you."

I liked part of that statement, so I had a cup—and it *was* strong. Ernie just smiled. "Make yourself comfortable. Nature calls, and I shall return momentarily."

When he returned, I mumbled something about the coffee not being the only thing that was strong. Then I asked him, "Ernie, what do you think of deceit?"

"Deceit," Ernie began in an authoritative voice, "was quite comfortable." Silence ensued, but I couldn't suppress a grin. "Deceit," he began again, "is the difference between a wannabe leader and a true leader. It all starts from within. You cannot lead others if you cannot lead yourself. It is extremely important to think of

the other person and his or her needs, not just what *you* want."

"In other words, you're only fooling yourself," I added.

"Not me," said Ernie, "but that's a nice cliché that fits what I am trying to say. The question is, 'would *you* follow you'?"

The tone of the conversation was getting serious—but this is what I had come over for, strong coffee or not. "I'm not sure I follow," I said.

"That's the point. It's pretty hard to get others to follow you, if you wouldn't follow yourself. You can't say one thing and then do another—people see right through it. Then the excuses start."

"Well, *excuse* me."

"You're excused," said Ernie, "but you don't have to leave if you don't want to."

I took the bait. "So how do you know if you want to follow yourself?" I asked.

"Well," he began, "you could start by getting feedback from others. But think of it this way: you need to be the leader of yourself, and see how it feels. Can you do all the things for yourself that you are supposed to do? Are you clear on your values and what your passion is? Unless you are clear, you wouldn't want to follow you, would you?"

"I think I'm starting to get it," I said. "If I'm going to be the leader of myself, I guess that also means I have to follow myself."

"Exactly. And when you follow yourself, you'll know whether you see a leader, or a horse's ass."

I chuckled, but I didn't think it was so funny. "I suppose if I see a horse's ass, I'm really just deceiving myself and others, if I claim to be a leader."

Ernie did not reply. He simply poured more coffee and put ample fixings in it. Then he stirred it for a long time. Finally he spoke. "I once was traveling and met up with a young lad named Dale at this small town café, who had just learned a life lesson from his grandfather. He told me the story, and it went something like this:

> My grandfather told me that a terrible fight was going on inside him. It was between two wolves: one was bad and full of anger, envy, greed, false pride, and arrogance. The other was good and full of kindness, love, humility, peace, and generosity. He told me that every person, including me, has such a fight going on inside him. So I asked him which wolf would win, and he simply replied, "The one you feed."

"The lad then told me he could relate very much to his grandfather's story, and that the advice had been invaluable to him."

"I think your coffee will kill both wolves inside me," I mused.

"Now, is that kind?" asked Ernie.

"Yes," I replied, "especially if it gets rid of the big bad wolf. But I don't mean to make light of your story, or the grandkid's—I think I am learning something here. Tell me, do you have to be *the best* at something to lead others at it?"

"Heck, no!" shouted Ernie. "Look at all the examples of coaches in professional sports. In fact, sometimes *the best* don't make good coaches or leaders at all. The same goes for politics, war, and business. What you *do* need is to be the best at bringing out the best in others, and again, it starts with you. The first step is to truly know yourself and what your passion is. Then live up to your values. No one's perfect, but the leader who admits mistakes and moves on is a lot more credible than the one who tries to cover it up. The cover-up guy is the definition of self-deceit. It's usually obvious—if not immediately, then it is over time. It's when you tell those little white lies to cover up your own flaws."

"An example, please?" I asked, in the most pleasant of voices.

"OK," said Ernie. "I advocate 'think-time,' but it really seems to be taboo in most organizations."

"Is that what you are doing so often with your eyes closed?" I asked.

Ernie appeared a bit bothered now. He raised his voice slightly (which was not at all like him), and said, "Well, here's the difference, smarty-pants. You'll know if I'm *productively* thinking when I am able to tell you about new ideas or solutions to issues. And you'll be especially interested when they are solutions for *you*."

"Oh," was all I could mutter.

"Yeah, 'oh' is right," Ernie continued. "But, if instead of solutions, I tell you, 'This is one of the seven habits of highly effective people,' or 'I'm in the management training program,' or some other cover-up, then it's just a little white lie and I'm only betraying myself. Even if you know I'm just kidding—I have failed as a leader and have not owned up to it."

"This has been helpful, Ernie. I think I should leave now and let it sink in. I would like to say I'll have some more of your coffee, but then I would be only betraying myself," I said, without an ounce of sarcasm.

3

The Five Percent Solution

I STOPPED BY Ernie's recently, because I had run into a number of challenges at work, all having to do with people: when to hire, who to hire, and how to keep them. It was Saturday morning and I could smell the coffee. I knocked on the door, but there was no answer. I knocked again and got the usual reply: "When you're tired of knocking, come on in."

I wondered if I would ever learn. Nevertheless, I walked in.

"Coffee?" asked Ernie.

"Coffee," I replied.

"Are you just repeating after me, or do you actually want a coffee?" Ernie asked, grinning.

“Both,” I said. I was enjoying the conversation so far.

“So what brings you here so early on a Saturday morning, my friend? You should be home with your family,” Ernie said in a rather friendly tone.

“Yes, I know—I should be at home, but I feel extremely challenged at work these days, and I thought if I could get some ideas, I would then be more relaxed and tuned in to my kids.”

“I’ve been many places and worked with many people, some of whom were full of ideas. Therefore, I am somewhat of an idea expert. Do you get the idea?” Ernie asked.

“Not yet,” I replied, “but I sense I will get it very soon.”

“Tell me why you feel so challenged at work.”

“It’s the people, Ernie. Don’t get me wrong. A lot of them want to do a great job, and a good portion of that group actually does a good job. But there seems to be this entitlement mentality for benefits, compensation, inspiring work—the list goes on and on. I really don't know what makes people tick," I replied dejectedly.

"Do people claim to be overworked?"

"All the time. And it is busy now—we're all working flat out," I replied, hoping this was just the easy answer.

"Many years ago," Ernie began, "I felt very tired and overworked myself. I blamed it on the company, the economy, the unions, and even some of my co-workers, who seemed to have it made in the shade. Then I thought it might be me, so I blamed it on iron-poor blood, lack of vitamins, dieting, and several other maladies. But then I discovered the real reason."

"Really," I said, hopeful that I would get a good idea from Ernie today.

"Yes, really. I found that I was doing everything…for everybody. Listen closely," Ernie said, cupping his hand to his ear. "The population of this country is about 33 million, and 10 million are now retired. That leaves 23 million to do all the work. There are 15 million in schools of some sort or another, so that leaves 8 million to do all the work. Then, 3 million are paid by the federal government, so that leaves 5 million to do all the work. I guess I should say all the *real* work. About half a million are in the armed forces, so that leaves 4.5 million to do all the work. If you look at all the provincial and municipal bureaucracies, that takes out another 2.3 million, so that leaves 2.2 million to do all the work. I would say there are about 1.6 million children who are not yet in school, so that leaves 600,000 to do all the work. There are 47,000 in hospitals, so now we only have 553,000 to do all the work. Today there are 552,998 unemployed people, so that leaves just two people to do all the work."

"Wow," I said, trying not to look impressed.

"Yeah, wow," said Ernie, "that means you and me. And you're coming here whining about *people* challenges. Seems to me you should just join the unemployed, but then that would leave me with all the work!"

"I'm not really whining, Ernie. But you make a good point: so often we ask people to help out, and the response is, 'I'm too busy.'"

"Actually, that's not a bad response," said Ernie. "But I have found, in my extensive travels, that people who are passionate about what they do rarely use that excuse. Everybody's busy in some way, shape, or form—it's really a matter of priorities."

"So what you are saying is that if you stick to the priorities, progress can be made, and people should be busy," I said.

"Yes. You want people to be busy, and you want them to be busy with the right things. So you have to know the right time to hire, and who to hire."

Now he was getting to the crux of what was really bothering me. "Ernie, there seem to be so many schools of thought on that topic. Some people say, 'Hire now based on forecasted needs for growth.' Others say, 'Hire after you get the business or hit certain targets—then be prepared to manage a little chaos.' Then there are those who say, 'Hire to fix problems, and then fit the people into a growing business.' This can get very confusing, because each idea has some merit on its own," I said, growing more perplexed as I went on.

"When you have wisdom, none of this stuff is really that complex. In my travels, I believe I have acquired such wisdom. It wasn't always that way, and I have made my share of mistakes, but I can help you now. Some people think they have all the answers, but they really don't. For example, do you know why lemon juice is made with artificial flavor, and dish-washing liquid with real lemons?"

I could see his stomach jiggling as he suppressed a laugh, so I said nothing.

"The solution to your little dilemma is simple," Ernie began. "I call it 'the five percent solution.'"

After the usual moment of silence, he had piqued my curiosity, so I asked the inevitable, "What do you mean by 'the five percent solution'?"

"Always run your organization with five percent less people than you believe you really need. Some people call this lean, but I think it keeps people jazzed. Lean thinking should be applied to the waste in the processes, not to the number of people you have."

"Interesting. Tell me more." I was now thinking about some opportunities back at work.

"When you have five percent less people than you really need, your employees will be forced to prioritize better. Of course, you will have to help some people with this more than others, and you will have to encourage their ideas to improve processes. You see, if you run too lean with people, they will be overwhelmed and too frustrated to manage priorities well. And you, as the leader, will be spending all your time putting out fires. But with just five percent less, it's manageable—no one should ever be standing around idle, at least not if you have created good teamwork—but we can talk about teamwork another day."

As I was processing this wisdom, so many questions were popping into my head, so I asked Ernie the first one that came to mind: "How do you lead everyone to the same goal, when they are not all at the same level of proficiency with their tasks?"

"Good question, young man. You cannot lead everyone the same way; you can't even lead one person the same way for everything they do. Think about your five most critical tasks or roles. Is it not true that you excel at some, with no input needed from anyone, yet with others you may need some encouragement to gain more confidence?"

I thought about my roles, and the answer was obvious. "Yes," I said, with a bit of a smile.

"And I'll bet there may even be some tasks that are new, given our growing company, and you simply need to learn the step-by-step process," Ernie continued.

"Yup."

"So you need to provide different leadership for each person, for each role they do. This doesn't mean you single-handedly have to do all this: you can line up the right help based on their readiness for any task or role. Eventually you coach them to where they just do it, do it well, and keep you informed as necessary. This means they let you know about both the good news and the bad news."

"That sounds like I need to communicate well in order to understand everyone's needs." I was now starting to get the picture.

"You're catching on. Not bad for someone who's not too well-traveled."

Just as I was starting to feel good about how I was going to organize my people, another challenge hit me—right in the gut. "This is great," I said, "but what if you are at that magic level of five percent less people than you need, but you don't really have the *right* people?"

"Hmmm," was the response. I waited.

Finally he spoke again. "This will be a process that takes time. The motto is, 'Be slow to hire and quick to fire.' If you have the wrong people on the team, and there is not a productive place for them elsewhere, you need to let them go. Then be careful and deliberate when you do hire—always. In busy times this is hard to do, but just throwing a 'warm body' at a problem when it's hectic will kill you."

"I've made that mistake—very costly," I said.

"Hire smart people, and 'smart' is not defined by IQ, either."

"What do you mean?" I asked.

"Well, the opposite of a smart person is an idiot. Being an idiot is a choice. Someone could have a very high IQ, but choose to behave like an idiot. So look for people who have a good work ethic—that would be smart on your part—and make sure they are friendly. These people will be eager to learn, so you can train, train, train. This is extremely important: if you want things to improve, you have to train your people. The good ones—the smart ones that is—will get the training they need and want anyway, whether you offer it or not. If you want them to stay with you and your company, you need to be the one giving it. And then make sure you recognize their efforts when they start making improvements."

"Lots to think about," I said. "But now I have a game plan, so it's time to go have some fun with my family."

"You didn't finish drinking your coffee," Ernie said in a commanding tone.

"Actually, it was *your* coffee—you made it. Finish it if you like."

I went home.

4

Teamwork is Dangerous

I WOKE UP the other day in a good mood: I was going to be traveling to the field again with Ernie, and would have plenty of windshield time to pick his brain. We were taking my truck this time, so I stopped at Timmy's to grab some coffee—I knew Ernie's favorite was a "double-double."

When I arrived at Ernie's, he was waiting for me. He jumped into the truck and grabbed his coffee. "What did you get me?" he asked, before he even saw the coffee. "I smell something good."

"It's not me," I replied, "but it could be the 'double-double' I got you."

"You're a good man!" he exclaimed. "Now let's get on the road."

We were heading up north to a remote field location, and I knew the drive would be about six hours. "Have you ever been to these parts before?" I asked, not really sure of how extensive his travels have been.

"I've traveled to many places and seen many things. This area is one of them. Therefore I have good insight on the best way to get there, and what to expect once we arrive."

"Good," I said. "I'll follow your directions. I have much to talk to you about today."

Ernie looked out the window, but before he turned away, I could see a grin starting to crease his face. After a minute or so he said, "The other day I arrived at work earlier than usual. When I went up the hall past Barney's office, I noticed his door was open, so I poked my head in to say 'hello,' and guess what I saw?"

I knew Ernie would outlast me if I didn't take the bait, so I took it: "I couldn't begin to guess. What did you see?"

"I saw him kissing his secretary, who I know is his girlfriend of two years. This really caught me by surprise, and angered me as well, so I shouted, 'Is this what I pay you for?' He quickly replied, 'No, sir, I do this free of charge.' I couldn't help but laugh and walk away."

Not knowing whether to believe the story or not, I just smiled and nodded.

"I've been thinking a lot lately about the importance of teamwork," I began.

Ernie didn't let me get too far. He quickly responded by saying, "Teamwork is dangerous."

This caught me by surprise. After all, we were establishing teams all over the company, and certainly there were examples from all walks of life, especially sports, that would appear to counter what Ernie was suggesting.

"I came across a quote by Vince Lombardi that would suggest otherwise," I retorted.

"You can suggest all you want," said Ernie, "but the proof is in the results. So what is the quote?"

I gladly recited, "'Individual commitment to a group effort—that is what makes a team work, a company work, a society work, a civilization work.'"

"Well, I suppose Vince has a good point," replied Ernie, "but if that individual commitment is self-serving and not for the group, bad things can happen. It will be up to the leader to make sure all individuals understand, and are focused on, a common goal."

Now we were getting somewhere. Ernie was surely about to enlighten me with some of his profound knowledge. And I wasn't disappointed.

"People always talk about the importance of teamwork," started Ernie. "They play up the importance, usually through sports analogies, and the next thing you know, teamwork gets a bad rap in the workplace—like it's just a bunch of nonsense."

"You're right, Ernie!" I exclaimed. "So often I hear people saying, 'He's not a team player,' or, 'She's only concerned about her own team, and not the whole department.' Yet I know these same people were great team players in sports as they were growing up. What the hell explains that?" I asked, anticipating Ernie's response.

"Well," started Ernie, "I see three main reasons. Firstly, the individual's commitment is often to the individual, not the team. Examples are everywhere: the salesperson who steals accounts and hoards information for himself, or the hockey star who is more concerned with how many goals he scores than how many wins the team has."

"I can see that," I said. "So what's the second reason?" Now I was getting interested.

"The individual's association with the group can be so strong that 'groupthink' drags the team down. There was once a psychologist named Solomon Asch who did a bunch of experiments on human beings," said Ernie, in his professorial voice.

"I hope you're not going to tell me something cruel," I jumped in, not really believing that this was where Ernie was headed.

"No, not at all," replied Ernie, seemingly unaware of my sarcasm. "His experiments showed that 70 percent of the time, people will agree with the group, even when the group is clearly wrong!"

"That would explain a lot of mediocrity," I said. "Not to mention a lot of excuses seeking to explain the mediocrity."

"Yes. Now listen carefully. The third reason has to do with authoritarian leadership, which, like it or not, is still very prevalent in the workplace today. Another psychologist, Milton Rokeach, said that people who like hierarchies seem to be comfortable giving orders."

"I've seen lots of that, even in our company. But not from you, Ernie."

"Sure you have—it's rather normal, given the history of organizations and despite ongoing attempts to change it. But here is what is really interesting: those same people who like giving orders—they also like taking orders! They seem to thrive on hierarchy. They also tend to be close-minded about new ideas and problem-solving. Open-minded personalities are freethinkers who dislike authority and seek new solutions. Given that many organizations promote authoritarian personalities to leadership positions, there's a built-in obstacle to effective teamwork."

"Wow! So what can we do to start fixing it?"

"I think we need to look at some examples where this hasn't occurred, then keep telling the story," replied Ernie, almost as if he expected the question.

"I'm assuming you have a story?" I stated it like a question.

"Yes, I do," Ernie replied.

After the usual minute of silence, I couldn't stand it any longer, so I made my demand: "Would it be possible for you to tell me the story before we finish this trip?"

"I thought you'd never ask," said Ernie. "Seems there was a fellow by the name of Jack McBride who used to run dogsleds to transport cargo between towns, back in the 1930's. An important thing you should know is that

Jack emigrated from Scotland and had no previous experience running these huskies. But he wanted to make a few bucks, so he dedicated himself to learning the trade, and most importantly, to understanding the dogs."

"Like a leader making sure he understands his people," I chimed in.

"You catch on fast. But the best is yet to come. One day in 1935 there was a plane crash near Peerless Lake. No one was killed, but the plane needed some parts before they could get it airborne again. The nearest place to get the parts was Slave Lake, so they asked Jack if he could run his dogs from Peerless to Slave and back again. Of course they offered him a bonus to make the trip in less time than usual. So Jack took up the offer and headed off. Now this is amazing: he made the round trip in six days!" exclaimed Ernie.

"Six days? That sounds like a hell of an accomplishment, but help me put it into perspective. What would that distance be?"

"Well, it's damn near three hundred miles, with today's roads. Now maybe Jack took a more direct route back then, but think of the terrain. And let me tell you, there was a ton of snow in those days."

I could hardly believe it. Given my mathematical prowess, I came to a quick conclusion: "That would be like doing two marathons a day for six days in a row. Those dogs must have been exhausted!"

"I would think so, but wait, there's more," Ernie said.

"Carry on," I begged.

"Well, I actually met Jack in 1974 and at that time, I knew that he held this world speed record for running a dogsled team, which, by the way, he still holds today. So I asked him what the secret to his success was. He told me there were two things that made his dog teams more effective than the competition's."

"I notice he answered your question by saying what made the *team* effective, rather than what made *him* effective," I interjected.

"Good point," Ernie said. "He couldn't have done it himself. Now, if you look at the history of dogsledding, you will find that 'mushing,' as they call it, always made use of a dog whip or mushing whip. For thousands of years it was assumed that this would motivate dog teams to greater efforts in hauling loads from place to place in harsh conditions. But Jack McBride had a different opinion and that was his first secret: he never whipped his dogs. Early on, he had realized that when you whip a team, it actually tends to slow the dogs down, because instead of concentrating on the trail ahead, they are always looking over their shoulders, waiting for that whip to crack."

"And the second secret?" I was now getting really interested.

"This is the truly amazing part. Jack's second secret was that he believed he should never add to the dogs' workload. Instead, he always ran beside his sled, sharing the trail and motivating his dogs. Because he never rode on the sled, he never added to their workload. The dogs actually saw it as a game—they didn't want their leader, Jack, to outrun them!"

"You mean Jack himself ran almost three hundred miles in six days through the snow? When did he have time to eat or...," I started to ask.

"I know what you're thinking," interrupted Ernie. "And remember, Jack was only 5'8" and he had a huge chest—must've been from running so much. But let's focus on the teamwork. Can you imagine a leader who never 'whipped' his team? And never intentionally added to their workload for the sole purpose of making things easier for himself?"

On reflection I could think of a couple of bosses throughout my career who had "whipped" me. The fear of reprisal made me work, but never to a highly productive level. Maybe I was too afraid of making a mistake. And the same bosses were always dumping extra work on me, usually with no explanation. But worst of all, I knew I had done the same thing.

"Gee, Ernie. When you put it that way, I feel kind of guilty myself," I confessed.

"I suppose I do, too, but guilt is only bad if you don't do anything about it. Jack's story has had a huge impact on me. If you can't lead a team to be all working together, being creative, and not worried about the next crack of the whip, well, then...."

This time I interrupted Ernie. "Then teamwork is dangerous. I get the picture."

We drove on in silence for quite awhile.

5

How About a Free Lunch?

WOW! IT WAS Saturday morning already—amazing how quickly the week had flown by. I had so much to do around the yard, but it was only 7:30 a.m.—a great time to have a quick coffee with Ernie. So I walked on over and sure enough, there he was, sitting on the porch with a big cup of coffee.

“Good morning, Ernie!” I exclaimed, as I truly was glad to see him.

“Good morning, indeed!” he fired back. I knew right then we would have a good chat. “Want some coffee?” he asked.

“I assume you’re offering it for free,” I replied.

“I sense your cynicism,” said Ernie, “but that really is a point worth exploring if you want to succeed in life. You do want to succeed, don't you?"

Unsure of how to respond without either seeming cynical or becoming the butt of a famous Ernie joke, I hesitated for about fifteen seconds, and then chose the former. "And you have just the insight for this life lesson?" I asked.

"I've been many places and seen many things. This has allowed me to talk to many people, and I have therefore gained much wisdom. That indeed gives me the insight to provide you with your much needed lesson," stated Ernie.

I did feel he had something to tell me, so I remained calm, and then, in a polite voice, I asked, "Can I still have a coffee?"

"Of course you can, and it is free," said Ernie. "Not to mention it's damn good, too. So make yourself comfortable, I'll go get you a cup and we'll have a good chat."

I did as instructed, and Ernie came back with a steaming cup of hot coffee. And it was good.

Much to my surprise, Ernie did not wait for my request to get on with it. Instead he stated, "There ain't no such thing as a free lunch. Some people refer to this as TANSTAAFL."

Then the usual silence kicked in. I knew this was my cue to wait the customary sixty seconds (*man*, it can be painful), and then ask a question. So I did. "Is TANSTAAFL a widely use term?" I queried.

"Yes it is. And if you do one of your silly searches on the Internet, you will find there is quite a history and many opinions as to its origin. But I'll save you the time: the phrase actually refers to the once-common tradition of saloons that would provide a 'free lunch' to

customers, as long as they bought at least one drink. Then people caught on to the fact that they usually spent more for their 'free lunch' than if they went in and just paid for their lunch in the first place. However, most people seemed happy with this—maybe that's the same rationale for 'happy hour'—so the tradition continues to this day."

If it weren't early Saturday morning, I would have suggested going to the local saloon to get lunch and test the theory. Instead, I tried to get the real point out of Ernie—there was always a real point. "What does this have to do with my life lesson and my 'free' coffee?" I asked.

"Well," began Ernie, "I really believe in TANSTAAFL, except when it comes to *true* leaders. And I emphasize *true* leaders, because I have found that *most* people who think they are leaders really don't get it. In my travels, I once met a lady by the name of Kim, and she really emphasized to me the importance of this."

"Keep going," I insisted, now getting quite interested.

"She told me that true leaders do not expect anything in return," stated Ernie. He paused for several moments to let that sink in. "When you expect something in return, that would be classified as an investment. Some investments pay off, some don't. But when you give selflessly, not expecting anything in return—that is being a true leader. So I could not help but agree with her."

I waited awhile; Ernie lit a pipe and refreshed our coffees. As soon as I collected my thoughts I spoke. "Ernie," I started in a softer than normal voice, "don't leaders hope that their efforts to help others will lead to better productivity and growth for their companies?"

"Is this a trap?" retorted Ernie.

"Are you trying to help me right now?" I queried. "Because if you truly are, then that would mean you are being a leader. If you are trying to annoy me, then that is selfish and you are not being a leader."

Ernie did not respond. After the usual minute of silence, I couldn't stand it anymore, so I continued. "If a leader hopes that others will be more productive, or become better people, or whatever, then you could argue that he is really helping people with his own motives in mind. Therefore, the person receiving the leadership is not getting a 'free lunch.' So your TANSTAAFL theory even applies to *true* leaders," I stated. I was quite proud of my logic and expected Ernie to get very riled up. After all, he has traveled many places and seen many things, and his wisdom is second to none.

But instead he remained calm. "I know you respect my wisdom, for I have been many places. So listen carefully." I knew right then that I should. Ernie continued, "If a leader believes he can help someone become a better person or be more productive, and he does so for those reasons alone, then the pay-off is for the other person, not himself. If he tries to help someone only to help himself, then that is selfish—that is not being a *true* leader and I would even suggest it borders on manipulation. So you see, it really is a mindset."

"A mindset?"

"If your hearing is impaired, I will repeat myself for your benefit," said Ernie. "Yes—a mindset. It is all a matter of purpose and intent. If you *expect* something in return, you are at best investing, maybe even manipulating, to get what you want. True leaders have an abundance mentality and give to others selflessly, expecting nothing in return. The amazing thing is, history has shown that the end results of true leadership are always greater than could ever be imagined. And leaders foolish enough to think that if they conceal their profit-seeking motives by acting as if they are being selfless 'givers,' find that people eventually see through this act and then it all backfires on them."

I took a sip of coffee, actually, a gulp of coffee. "This is getting pretty deep!" I exclaimed.

"How could it be getting deep when you keep drinking it?" Ernie chortled. I knew that one was coming as soon as I said it. As his belly jiggled, he continued, "It's really not that deep when you think about it. You just have to do things for the right reasons."

With that, I realized maybe I had just drunk a free coffee. If Ernie was the leader I thought he was, he should have expected nothing in return. And he didn't.

"Let me tell you the story of a manager I once knew who really didn't get it," said Ernie.

"Please do," I said.

"An eager young employee had been working extra hard for several months. Now this employee was a bit of a renegade: he did not dress according to company protocol and kept his hair extremely long. He decided to ask his boss, who portrayed himself as a religious man, if they could discuss the possibility of a company vehicle. His boss took him to his office and said to him, 'I'll make a deal with you: you finish the current project on-time and on-budget, *and* get your hair cut—*then* we'll talk about it.' After about a month, the young man came back and asked his boss if they could now discuss a company vehicle. His boss said, 'Young man, I've been really pleased with your work and accomplishments. You brought the project in on-time and on-budget, and the company has made a considerable profit. But you did not get your hair cut!' The young man thought for a moment and then replied, 'You know, sir, I've been thinking about that. As a religious man yourself, you know that Samson had long hair, Moses had long hair, Noah had long hair, and even Jesus had long hair.' To which his boss replied, 'Yes, and they walked everywhere they went!'"

I had a good laugh, and then said, "I think I'm getting the picture. Thanks for the lesson and the coffee."

I went home.

6

Lean Thinking

I HAD JUST arrived at work, about an hour early, as usual. Just as usual was the fact that Ernie was already there, had made the coffee, and was on his second cup. I thought this would be a good time to pick his brain a little, as I had some ideas on how to improve the way we did some jobs.

“Good morning, Ernie,” I said with a smile.

“Yes, it is a good morning, indeed,” replied Ernie, always the optimist (even though sometimes he pretended not to be). “With that smile, I know you have something on your mind—have a seat.”

“As a matter of fact, I do have something on my mind,” I said enthusiastically. “I believe I have some ideas that can help our company.”

"I'll be damned," said Ernie.

This caught me off-guard, so I waited thirty seconds, and then asked, "What makes you say that?"

Ernie, with a serious look on his face, said, "I like the way you said, '*our* company'; we're all in this together. I met the president of a mid-cap oil company recently and I believe he thought the company was *his*, which doesn't do much for teamwork, does it?"

"Of course not," I shot back. "What makes you believe he thought the company was his?"

"Because," said Ernie, "after a tour of one of their facilities, he asked me, 'How do you like my company so far?'"

"What did you say?" I quickly asked.

"I said, 'I don't like your company, so I think I'll go and visit with somebody else,'" said Ernie.

I have to admit, it took a minute before it sunk in, and Ernie did a good job of concealing his smile. But his jiggling belly eventually gave it away. After a polite laugh, I started my exposition.

"I have been studying the concept of 'Lean Thinking,'" I began. "It's a way of looking at work processes and getting rid of the 'muda,'" I said, with a hint of self-importance. I waited patiently for some sort of response from Ernie; the long lull in conversation was becoming painful, and, in my opinion, unproductive. 'Muda,' in fact. But Ernie finally spoke.

"I've been many places and seen many things, but I have never heard of this 'muda.'

Therefore, to me, it means nothing," Ernie replied, almost triumphantly.

"No, Ernie; nothing means nothing." (I thought this was clever—a double play on words). "In your vast travels, you must have skipped Japan. In Japanese, 'muda' means 'waste.' So that is actually the opposite of 'nothing,'" I retorted. I must have sounded almost pompous to this man of wisdom.

"Well, now," Ernie said with a hint of polite sarcasm. "You have my attention and my interest. Explain this 'Lean Thinking' and 'muda' to me, and how it can help our company."

"'Lean Thinking' is really a culture within an organization. I spent considerable time with a fellow who implemented this in his organization over the past seven years. He says the first thing to stress is that 'lean' does not mean less people," I said.

"I'm glad you said that," said Ernie. "That would be a likely perception, if you ask me."

"Yes, and you really need someone at a senior level to champion the whole thing, in order to remove any fear. This is where leadership comes in," I explained.

"So what can leadership actually do, besides be a cheerleader?" asked Ernie.

"Good question. This is where the concept of 'muda' comes in: there is waste in almost every process you care to look at. The problem is, most people don't want to admit they create waste while they are working away at a process. It's always easier to point out the waste in someone else's work. But the real progress comes when people have the humility to look at their own work, or their work as part of a team, and eliminate 'muda.' So to answer your question, I think the best thing a leader can do is show everyone some of the waste that he or she has created."

"That would be a disgusting start to the day," chuckled Ernie.

"Not that kind of waste!" I fired back. "I doubt if there is a work process today that doesn't have some waste in it. This could be in terms of steps in the process, delays, improper equipment or materials, lack of understanding or skill—the list goes on. This would be the case for the office, the shop floor, or heck, even in sales. In fact, I was reading a book by Jeffrey Gitomer—you know, the big sales guru—and he says ninety-five percent of salespeople don't follow their own processes correctly."

"No kidding," said Ernie. "And I wouldn't just pick on salespeople. I've never met an engineer who did anything right. In fact, they all wear an iron ring just to remind us of that! Anyway—back to why a leader should show his people his own waste."

"Yeah, it's really the humility thing, Ernie. I believe that if the leader steps up and says, 'Here's something I've been doing for some time, and I've analyzed it and found a better way to do it,' then people will start to open up and focus on the waste that they create as well.

"And if you follow the old 80/20 rule, there is likely some low hanging fruit that would allow for a couple of quick hits. In other words, even though we believe there is waste in every single process, it's probable that 80 percent of the waste is in 20 percent of the processes. Some of this will be obvious, and quick changes can be made to get some early success," I explained.

"Can you give me an example of a success that you have come across in your studies?" queried Ernie.

"Sure. I have been talking to the COO of one manufacturer. He said they were able to reduce the time-to-manufacture on components from eleven hours down to forty-five minutes. Of course, when they did this, there was a lot of fear of pink slips coming down the line. But the message that everyone in the company got—from the owner—was, 'If you work with us on "Lean," you will always have a job—maybe not the same job—but indeed a job.'

"He also told me that you can't make 'Lean' work if your management insists on leadership through a hierarchy. It's got to be done situation by situation, and people have to feel empowered: let them do their own quality checks along the line, be responsible for the output, things like that. The only people who were negatively affected were those who refused to get on board with the concept," I stated.

"So I gather that if we wanted to implement this 'Lean Thinking,' we would need to start by making sure our leadership was on board, not bound by chain-of-command thinking, and open to leading people situationally," said Ernie.

"That would be a must," I replied.

"I'm sold," said Ernie. "Let me gather the senior team here and see what kind of response we get."

I went back to my office, feeling rather proud. Ernie had a way of making you feel good when you brought up a new idea.

7

Happy People

FINALLY, THE WEEKEND had arrived! It was not a matter of dreading work, not by a long shot. I actually enjoyed my work and the people in it. The weekend was just that—a nice ending to a great week. And this weekend I was going fishing on Saturday with Ernie. I arrived at his door at about 5:00 a.m., all ready to go. Ernie was ready and graciously accepted the "double-double" I had brought him.

"It's gonna be a great day!" exclaimed Ernie. "My gear is in the garage. Let's get it in your Jeep and get the show on the road."

"You bet," I said, and we were off. Ernie was a seasoned fisherman, and we had our favorite place in the mountains. It was just a little creek, and Ernie had named it twenty years ago. He simply called it "The Little Creek"—a beautiful place, from where we would always come back with a bag of pan-fry trout. It was about a two-hour drive, so we would have plenty of time to chat.

I had been thinking a lot over the past week about the company that we both worked for, and the low employee turnover the company enjoyed. There was no question that the loyalty of our employees showed up when dealing with customers, which in turn showed up in our profits. "Ernie," I began, "we really have a good thing going with so many employees staying with the company, when we know there are loads of opportunities out there for them. Don't you think we're lucky?"

Ernie thought for a few moments and took a rather large gulp of coffee. "It never ceases to amaze me that whenever someone is successful, others will say he was 'lucky.' So I just agree with them," said Ernie in a matter-of-fact way.

I felt there had to be more, so I took the bait. "Why would you just agree with them?"

"You see," said Ernie, "success actually *is* luck—just ask any failure."

I smiled and thought, "Good point!"

Ernie continued, "You need to look at all the things we are doing to create loyalty. I've always believed you have to show loyalty before you can get loyalty. This starts with our employees, not our customers—their loyalty is simply an outcome."

Good point—again. Now I was curious, so I asked Ernie to tell me more. He said, "It all starts at the point of hiring. Sure, we want technically competent people, that's a given. But the other thing to look for is *happy* people. Look at all the top talent we have—they're all happy, at least most of the time. And then we have to do everything we can to keep them happy. That is where loyalty comes in: happy people will follow the loyal actions you show."

“Sounds like a great recipe, but give me an example of a loyal action.” I anticipated Ernie would come up with a good one.

“An example would be how you talk about other people in this company when they are not present,” replied Ernie.

I thought about this for a minute, and when it sank in, it made perfect sense. Then I reflected on how the leadership of our company all followed the principles Ernie was talking about. A smile came to my face—I knew that I was *happy*. And it wasn’t just luck.

Ernie knew that I got it. So he couldn’t resist throwing in some more profound insight: “Keep in mind that we all make mistakes. Every man is a damn fool for at least five minutes every day. Leaders do not exceed the limit.”

“We’re almost at ‘The Little Creek,’” I said. “I know the fishing will be good, so we’ll have to be leaders and not exceed the limit!”

We both knew we were going to have a great day.

8

Humble Ice Cream

I KNEW ERNIE was very fond of ice cream. It was a hot summer day, and we had worked hard. As I passed by his office, I poked my head in and said, "Hey, if you're not doing anything this evening, we should go for a stroll and stop by Dairy Queen for an ice-cream treat."

"I've been many places and tried many things, and one thing I've learned is that ice cream on a hot day is hard to beat," said Ernie. "Not that I'm telling you how to manage your family, but feel free to bring your kids along. And by the way, there is a leadership message in that statement."

I waited for the message. Ernie had great listening skills—especially in getting others to listen to him. So, as usual, I had to ask: "And the message is?"

"Don't ask your kids if they want to go to Dairy Queen for ice cream when you know what the answer is," said Ernie.

"So when *should* you ask them, when you don't know what the answer is?" I retorted sarcastically.

"That was lame and I will choose to ignore it," stated Ernie. "My point is that you should first consult with your trusted advisors—in this case, your wife—in order to establish priorities. At work, that would be like asking all your employees if they want a raise, without first consulting those who manage your compensation plan."

"I see your point and will keep that in mind—at home and at work," I said. It really was a good point. Even though the compensation example was an obvious one, I could think of a lot more subtle examples that fit the same lesson. And God knows I might have gone home and asked my kids if they wanted to go to Dairy Queen before consulting my wife.

"Say, Ernie—," I stopped mid-sentence.

"'Ernie,'" said Ernie.

It took me a few seconds to get it. Then I politely chuckled and continued with my question. "I was recently asked by one of my employees how important it was for a leader to be humble. I struggled with the answer, because I've seen all sorts of personalities be successful in leadership roles. What are your thoughts?"

"Of course all sorts of personalities can be successful in leadership roles. This applies to business, the home, church, sports—you name it," replied Ernie.

"Hockey," I replied, not wanting to miss the chance for a little revenge.

"Touché," said Ernie. "But back to your point: 'humble' is a funny word. One dictionary definition says it means 'marked by meekness.' And if you look up 'meek,' it says 'showing patience and having a gentle disposition.' This could be a strong characteristic in certain situations. However, another definition for 'meek' is 'lacking spirit or backbone.' Seems to me this would not be good in any situation. Yet, many people see being humble as simply the opposite of being arrogant and wanting all the recognition. This *would* be good in *any* situation."

"I see your point, Ernie. I suppose a true leader knows when to speak up and make a decision, but also knows when to be 'humble'—by some positive definition—and give credit to the team."

Ernie nodded with approval. "I think the key point is to never let ego, as important as that is for self-esteem and leadership, get in the way. As in any walk of life, nobody is *that* good."

"I met the leader of a company recently, and I knew he had successfully run this company for twenty-five years, so I asked him to what he attributed his success. You know what he said?" I asked Ernie.

"I know many things, but in this case I would be guessing at the answer to your query," said Ernie. "Please continue, because I am interested in what he said."

"He said a lot of it was *luck*," I said with emphasis.

"Did you remind him there are two kinds of luck?" asked Ernie.

"Actually, I didn't," I continued, "but I did tell him that was bullshit. He didn't like that too much, but he said a few other things, too. He said he'd always had a thirst for learning, even as a young engineer. For example, he once took a demotion to do work he felt he would really enjoy and learn from. He also refused a great opportunity in another company to ensure his family stayed intact; he felt he couldn't be successful in his business life if he didn't strike a balance with his family life."

"I would say that this person has the humility to be a great leader. I would also say that the choices he made were those of a true leader, and that these choices have had a greater impact on his success than luck had. Remember, choice—not chance—determines destiny. For those who like to believe in luck, my advice is that you have to create the environment for luck to kick in. Sounds like your friend did just that," concluded Ernie.

"I didn't say he was my friend," I shot back.

"He is," was Ernie's final comment.

9

Selfless Leadership

I HAD SOME thoughts I wanted to share with Ernie, so I barged into his office one morning. "Hi, how are you?" I asked in a rush, eager to get to my story.

"I've been many places and seen many things—therefore I know many things. This means that I know, and am not guessing, when I say 'damn fine,'" replied Ernie. I did think he was sincere.

"And what has possessed you to feel so damn fine?" I asked, this time really wanting to know.

"Well—" Ernie began.

"Hold on," I interrupted, "that is a deep subject—you taught me that."

“Touché,” said Ernie. “I really do feel good, though. I just ate a piece of Mrs. McDougall’s fresh-baked bread, still warm out of the oven, and the butter, real butter, melted into it….” Ernie seemed to drift on in thought, enjoying the moment. I’d always admired how Ernie got so much satisfaction out of life’s little pleasures. It was a good reminder that I needed to stop and smell the roses once in awhile myself.

Ernie sensed the silence and spoke up. “So what brings you by today, young man?”

“Well—“ I started, thinking that I would get interrupted, but I didn’t. “I met a fine young lady the other day. Her name was Sarah; in fact, I think it still is. Anyway, she taught me a great leadership lesson.”

“Amazing what you can learn from a young lady. Apparently, all you have to do is listen. But carry on—you have my curiosity,” said Ernie.

“She told me of a time in the sixth grade when she was in a track meet. She excelled at long-distance running, and was in a race that included two of her friends, Brandy and Melissa. Both of these friends were also very good runners, but Brandy was the one Sarah really wanted to beat. They started the race and Sarah was clearly in first place at about the half-way point. Melissa was close enough behind Sarah to call out to her: 'Brandy is down! Brandy is down!'

"Still running, Sarah turned her head around and saw Brandy lying on the ground. Without hesitation, both girls left the race and ran back to Brandy to see what was wrong. When they reached her, they realized she was having an asthma attack, but luckily it didn't last long, and she recovered quickly. The girls helped her up, and the three of them walked across the finish line.

"In fact, they all received participation ribbons for crossing the finish line, but Sarah missed out on the coveted first-place ribbon!" I exclaimed, still feeling a sense of pride for these young ladies.

"One thing is certain," Ernie started, "this Miss Sarah is smarter than a fifth grader. But at a young age, she taught herself a valuable lesson. I assume she could have won the race?"

"She told me she knew in her heart that she had it in the bag, but it was simply more important to tend to her friend. A totally selfless act," I replied.

"And what did her coach say to her?"

"Amazingly, he didn't get mad, even though several adults were close by and could have tended to Brandy. He actually gave Sarah a higher mark on her final report card, and told her she would do well in life," I said.

"Another lesson in leadership—the coach who is all about leading people rather than just having to win. I knew from the start of this conversation that I was having a damn fine day. Let's not stop now—do you have time for Tim Horton's?" invited Ernie.

"Always," I replied with a smile.

10

A Real Human Being

I HAD BEEN thinking for some time about certain people, both in our company and in others, who seemed to have emerged as leaders. The interesting thing to me was that in each case, this had taken place over many years—ten years at least. When I thought back to our first encounters, I would not have guessed this eventual outcome. And over the years, these people never made a sudden, unexplainable leap into the big offices. It seemed to be an evolutionary thing—it just grew on them. Was it intentional or did it just happen?

I knew just the person to ask. So I walked over to Ernie's—it was 7:30 a.m. on a nice, bright, sunny Saturday.

When I arrived, I knocked on the door. After waiting a full minute and getting no response,

I knocked again. Then I heard his thundering voice, "Who's there?"

I took the opportunity and said, "Jock."

"Jock who?" asked Ernie.

"Jock Strap, the all-American ball carrier," I replied.

I was pleasantly surprised when he opened the door, grinning from ear-to-ear, and let me in.

"I've been many places and seen many things, therefore I know many things and many people. Now I can add one more to the people I know—Mr. Strap. And there is no doubt Mr. Strap is extremely important to about half the people in the world."

I was going to ask, "Which half?" but decided this had gone on long enough. I had come here for a reason.

Ernie seemed to read my thoughts. "So what brings you here today, my friend? Now, before you answer, take a seat at the kitchen table, and let me pour you a cup of coffee," he said, as he gestured me to the table.

Yes, the coffee. Always the coffee to stimulate thought. "Ernie," I began, "I have been reflecting on several people I've known over the years, who I believe have become true leaders. And not by just climbing the corporate ladder, but by really having a strong, positive influence on those who seem to *want* to follow them."

"You are a bright individual," stated Ernie.

"I appreciate the compliment," I said.

"So when you reflect on people, be careful not to burn them out," Ernie said with a grin.

A moment of silence.

"So what's your point?" asked Ernie.

"My point is that these people seemed to become leaders step-by-step. They were not born that way, and it looks like they took small but intentional actions over a period of years to get there," I explained.

"Good observation," said Ernie. "Let me tell you about my old friend, George. He seemed to be a leader to me when I met him over fifteen years ago. Yet today he seems different—

much more humble, in fact. So I asked George about his journey, and it was quite fascinating. But what really caught my attention was what he said, right up-front."

I knew I would have to observe the obligatory moment of silence, and then beg for more. After about a minute I stated, rather confidently, "Well, now you have *my* attention."

"Good, because this is important," stated Ernie. "What George said was, 'Now I'm a human being.' Of course my immediate reaction was just like the one I see on your face right now: wasn't he a human being the day he was born? But he then clarified his statement. He said he started out as a human being—loving life as a kid. But somewhere towards the end of adolescence, he stopped, and he became a human *doing*.

"Life became an endless loop of chasing the dollar and climbing the ladder. He did well, taking on lots of responsibility, not the least of which was managing hundreds of people.

And back to your earlier question about the evolutionary process of leadership: according to George, that's definitely the way it was. This intentional part was allowing time to reflect," continued Ernie.

"Remember what you said to me about 're-flecting,'" I chimed in.

"Touché," said Ernie. "George talked about the leaders he had been mentored by for over twenty-five years. Looking back, he realized he was 'doing' instead of 'being.' Once that realization sunk in, he understood the difference—true leaders believe in people, including themselves. Hard work and getting things done is important, at home and at work, but the difference between a 'human being' and a 'human doing' is the belief in people."

I was now spellbound. "Did he explain how he got to that space?"

"Part of it was that intentional reflection, learning from others and from himself. He said he had to look inward, deeper and deeper, and at times it got really uncomfortable. Then he had to take steps to change what he called 'toxic surroundings.' This meant some hard decisions to create the culture he felt was appropriate at work and at home, rather than being dragged down by others' shortcomings.

"And the biggest thing he said he did was to let go of his ego. Not his confidence—just the ego that kept him from believing in others. I could tell he was sincere—he is truly more humble today than back then," Ernie concluded with vivid expression.

I had lots to think about and knew it was time to leave. I saw a jar of pickled eggs on the counter. Ernie caught my eye and asked, "You want one?"

"Don't mind if I do," I replied.

"You can't beat a pickled egg," said Ernie, grinning.

I went home.

11

Are You Positive?

I WOKE UP quite early the other day and felt well rested, so I decided to head in to work. But of course there had to be a pit stop on the way in—Tim Horton's. I was really looking forward to a quiet cup of coffee; after all, it was certainly not busy at 5:15 a.m. I decided to be easy on the environment and not use the drive-through. I had plenty of time to sit down inside and enjoy the morning paper.

As I was sitting down, a head appeared from behind a newspaper, and there was Ernie, laughing to himself. I sat down at his table and asked him what was so funny.

"First of all, I had a feeling you would be here early today," started Ernie.

"Really," I said, trying not to make it sound like a question, but a statement of fact.

"Really," stated Ernie—now it was indeed a fact. "Some people call it karma, some say it's the law of attraction, and others say it's vibrations sent out over frequencies that we pick up in our subconscious. My belief is that they are all really saying the same thing, and that there is truth to the matter."

"Really?" I asked, now actually asking a question.

"Really," said Ernie—again, it was a fact. "There is too much evidence all around us to ignore it or pass it off as coincidence. I thought you would show up here early this morning, because I was thinking of you and the exciting projects we have coming up this year. And, that made me think of our next fishing trip. Then I thought, I can't wait to talk to you about these things, so I headed to this coffee shop, because I was up anyway. So when you walked in, I was not really surprised at all."

"Never mind projects and fishing right now, Ernie. This vibration thing's got my interest. You really believe that people send out vibrations from their body?" I asked.

"Yes, I do. Think back on times when you have walked into a meeting when people were already there and talking to each other. Didn't you feel you could tell right away, without hearing what was actually being said, what the atmosphere was like? Or a family gathering, or a sporting event, or a funeral, or, or, or?" Ernie asked.

"I think I get your point. People often use expressions like, 'I felt positive vibes in that meeting,' or 'She gave off negative vibes when she spoke.'"

"Well, it's not coincidence," said Ernie.

"Are you positive?" I asked.

"If you're asking whether I'm sure or not, I speak with the utmost confidence. I have travelled the globe and am therefore global in my knowledge. If you're asking about my state of mind, I shouldn't have to answer—you should be picking up the vibes," Ernie replied with conviction.

"I would say you are positive, on both counts. But tell me, can a person learn to be positive?" I asked.

"Yes. And about that, I am positive. One time you told me you learned a lesson on leadership from a young lady who went beyond the call of duty to support a fellow competitor."

"I recall the story well," I said.

"Well, I learned a lesson on positive thinking from a two-year-old!" Ernie exclaimed.

"You've got my attention."

"An old friend of mine actually told me the story. When his kids were younger and he had the duty of looking after them while his wife was out shopping, his two-year-old was playing with a hammer. As you can imagine, things could only go well for so long. The kid

ended up giving himself a real good whack on the thumb. So, after cleaning up the mess and bandaging things up, my friend asked the lad how he was doing. Still whimpering in pain, the young boy exclaimed, 'Dad, I'm lucky!' 'Lucky?' his dad responded. To which the boy said, 'Yeah, I'm lucky it wasn't my sucking thumb.'

"You hear all these bullshit sayings about the glass being half-full or half-empty, and about how some psychologist thinks he can figure you out. All you need to do is watch how people look at *real* situations. This boy was serious, not just a 'wannabe' positive kid. And this has carried him through life, according to his dad," Ernie said forcefully.

"Seems to me there is always a choice." I began to summarize what I had learned. "Even when you get in a rut; whether it's because of the wrong friends, or an inefficient process at work, there are always choices to get out. A starting point would be to look at any negative influences and get rid of them. When you do that, you become more attractive to the things and the people you want."

"You bet. Of course it's easier said than done, but if you do it one step at a time, it's always achievable," said Ernie.

Amazing what can happen over a cup of coffee, I thought to myself.

12

Walk a Mile in My Shoes

IT WAS A beautiful summer evening—very calm and serene. It had rained earlier, so everything smelled fresh, as well. I was taking advantage of it all by going for a long walk. This gave me some much needed think-time, and I had all sorts of ideas to run by Ernie. His house was only a couple of minutes away, so I headed on over.

I could hear the TV going, so I knocked, paused briefly, then let myself in.

"Come on in," said Ernie.

"Very funny. Any coffee left?" I asked.

"The pot never gets empty—you know that. Help yourself."

I didn't usually have coffee in the evening, but whenever I was at Ernie's it just seemed appropriate. So I poured myself a cup and sat down on the sofa.

"What brings you by?" asked Ernie.

"I was out for a long evening stroll—" I began.

"I like long strolls," Ernie interrupted, "especially when they are taken by people who annoy me."

"And…?" I asked, wondering whether to stay or go.

"And now you may continue what you were saying—I don't include you in that group of people," replied Ernie.

"Well, before I left for my stroll, I heard the Elvis song, 'Walk a Mile in My Shoes.' For the first time, I really listened to it closely, and then I couldn't help but think about it during my stroll. I think that song has a powerful message for people. Do you know the one I'm talking about?"

"I've been many places and seen many things, including Elvis himself. Therefore I can speak with great authority on that song, and perhaps shed a whole new meaning on it for you. Listen carefully, because here is the point: before you criticize a man, walk a mile in his shoes. This way, when you *do* criticize him, you'll be a mile away, *and* you'll have his shoes," Ernie said in a mock-serious tone.

"You are a clever man. Can I walk a mile in your shoes?" I asked.

"Yeah, yeah," said Ernie, "someday maybe you should, but for now I do have a story that you would like. But before I tell it to you, let's set the record straight: Joe South wrote that song, not Elvis. The King did, however, do a marvelous job of singing it with the emotion that it deserves."

"Good, the record is now straight, and so is the CD," I said.

Ernie shook his head at my wisecrack, but then took on a serious look and began his story. I sat back comfortably, took a sip of coffee, and listened intently.

"I once travelled west of here, and during my travels met a man by the name of Billy Drew—one of the kindest people you could ever meet. He did a ton for the community and had many stories to tell. And most importantly, he had a love for his family that was second to none. But Billy was met with an unfair challenge that took his life at a young age.

"He had touched the lives of many people, so some of his closest friends decided to make sure his young daughter, Tatum, received a little extra by raising money every year in her name. You should see some of the letters she has written to them, in thanks for this kindness—they tug pretty good at the old heartstrings. But then one year, one of the guys—Ches was his name—decided to take things to another level.

"He entered himself in a walk-a-thon that was designed to raise money for cancer. Then he approached Billy's wife and asked permission to borrow a pair of Billy's shoes, so that he could 'walk a mile' in them."

Ernie sat silently for a moment, and you could see the impact that just telling the story was having on him. I was deeply moved myself and said nothing.

After about a minute, Ernie continued. "She gave him permission and Ches was on his way to challenging as many people as he could to get involved. And it worked. Not only did he raise a good sum of money, he stirred the spirit of a lot of people with his theme. He's the only person I have ever known who took the song you've been thinking about, and literally followed its advice.

"I spoke with Ches a few months after the event and I asked him how he felt the day he was walking in Billy's shoes. He said it was a very proud feeling, yet eerie at the same time. He really just wanted to do Billy proud, but when he began walking, it felt like a much bigger responsibility. He gained a much deeper appreciation for what Billy must have gone through.

"Overall, the concept was tremendous and there was a true 'passing of the torch.'" Ernie finished, and again remained quiet.

I let the story sink in, and then finally broke the silence. "I guess you truly cannot know what someone is going through until you walk a mile in their shoes. How can we teach this to our leaders?"

"Good point. As a metaphor, walking a mile in someone's shoes is difficult to do. It takes extremely careful listening and empathy. And it has to be sincere—you can't fake empathic listening. True leaders know when and how to do this, and it can be taught," replied Ernie.

I knew we would have to come up with a plan to teach these concepts. Right then, I felt inspired and exhausted at the same time. I went home and shut my eyes....

13

Lessons from Golf

IT WAS A beautiful Friday morning in June. Ernie stopped by my office, poked his head in, and made a compelling statement: "Finish what you are doing and pack up. I have a tee time at 11 o'clock this morning."

"I thought you only drank coffee," I replied, but that didn't even get a grin out of him. I liked the game of golf, and sneaking off on a Friday would be a real treat.

"You've been working hard, and the proof is in the results for this quarter," said Ernie, never afraid to praise others and to give credit, rather than take it all himself. "A little time off and a game of golf will be good for the soul. Besides, you need someone to play golf with, and I believe that is my role."

So off we went to hit the links. Ernie had a membership at a country club close to the mountains. I loved going there—everyone was so friendly, and it was definitely my favorite course to play. Ernie was a pretty good golfer, and we always had a few friendly bets on the line, although I doubt if either of us had ever lost more than six bucks.

As we left the city limits, the conversation picked up. "You can learn a lot about people from the game of golf," Ernie began.

I said nothing, trying to test his patience.

After two minutes of silence, Ernie continued. "You have just given me the perfect example."

Now he did have my attention. "How so?" I asked.

"By remaining silent, some people would conclude that, either you are the shy, quiet type, or that you are some sort of moron with nothing to say," replied Ernie.

Again, I said nothing.

"But I know better. It's simply a competition with you, and you were testing my patience," Ernie stated triumphantly.

"You are very perceptive," I shot back. "But we are not playing golf right now, so what is your point?"

"I believe that the game of golf starts as soon as you head to the course. Your competitive spirit emerges, and that means we are going to have a great day. I'm really just tugging at you, my friend, but I sincerely believe that on the golf course, personalities come out which can teach you a lot about people," said Ernie, with a bit of a laugh this time.

"I'm sure you have many stories to tell," I said, looking to gain some wisdom.

"I've been many places and played many courses, therefore I have many such stories!" exclaimed Ernie. "Once upon a time, my business partners and I travelled a great distance to meet the owners of another company similar to ours. The real purpose was to begin negotiating a deal to merge our two firms, and we thought that a great way to start was over a game of golf.

"Now, you should know that this was about ten years ago, and none of us had what you would call a low handicap. Yet by the fourth hole, one of the owners from the other company was using foul language, actually banging his clubs on the tee box after an errant shot, and taking big gouges out of the earth. Not only did I feel this was extremely poor golf etiquette, but I also learned something about the person, and how he might react under pressure in a negotiation," Ernie summarized.

"And how did it play out?" I asked.

"If you mean the golf game, not so well for him, as you can imagine. If you mean the negotiation, it was terrible. The good news was that we found out in just one meeting that it was not going to work, mostly because of this gentleman's approach to the whole thing. The bad news was that he spoiled a perfectly good day of golf for several people." Ernie's eyes narrowed as he recalled the scene.

"So what do you think of competition in golf, if it brings out those ugly behaviors?"

"There's nothing wrong with competition in any sport, in any business, or in anything, for that matter. The point is that you need to remain in control of your emotions at all times," Ernie explained. "Look at you and me: we always play for a couple of bucks, kid each other while we play, and rarely do I even hear you swear. Not bad for a competitive person like yourself."

"Thank you," I said, graciously accepting the compliment.

So our game began. We decided to have a match play, straight up, even though Ernie's handicap was five strokes better than mine. Both of us started off well, and there was no one in front of us, so the pace was great. I was actually feeling quite relaxed, and very grateful for the break from work.

At the fourth hole, as we were walking down the fairway, Ernie said to me, "There are some damn good leadership lessons in this game."

This time I didn't wait to respond, mainly because if I didn't respond, I ran the risk of hearing about it midway through my putt. "Give me one," I fired back.

"Don't mind if I do," smiled Ernie. "I think the top of my list would be the lesson on honesty. Seems to me most people will claim that honesty is a personal value, and often want it included in the statement of their corporate values. Yet they go on to behave quite differently.

"Years ago, I was meeting with a client company, and two of their employees were there: one was the general manager, the other a sales rep. We were talking about the importance of having the word 'honesty' in their corporate values. The GM said it was of paramount importance that the word be included (by the way, this guy was one of the nicest people I've ever met). But the sales rep said they couldn't *say* they were honest and yet not live up to it. The GM challenged him to give an example.

"The sales rep told of a time when they had held a golf tournament, mostly for their clients, but there were also a few suppliers and landowners in attendance. Everyone there had put a business card in for a raffle for some prizes. When it came time for the last draw, and a chance to win a really nice golf bag, the company fixed it to make sure a client won," said Ernie, almost in disbelief.

"You've got to be kidding," I remarked.

"Are *you* kidding?" said Ernie. "The GM replied that this was not really dishonest, as the tournament was intended primarily for clients, and that it was only fair that one of them should win the grand prize."

"I wonder how he keeps score on the golf course?" I said.

"Who knows? But you're right, it does make you wonder. When it comes to honesty, the key is consistency. You can claim to be honest, but then come up with carefully planned exceptions. If I know a guy has cheated on his score in a golf game, I will certainly be suspicious as to how he conducts himself in business. Remember, nothing counts in a golf game like your opponent," Ernie said with a smile.

"Good point," I said. "Reminds me of a guy I knew by the name of Graham. One morning over breakfast his wife asked him why he never played golf with his co-worker, Gord, anymore. He said to his wife, 'Would you play golf with a man who talks when you're putting, bumps his ball in the rough, and shaves off a stroke here and there?' His wife said, 'Absolutely not!' Graham then said, 'Well, neither will Gord.'"

We both finished the fourth hole with a par. The game continued, and by the end of the ninth hole, Ernie was up by one.

"Looks like we have a pretty good competition going on here," I remarked.

"Competition can be a good thing, in sports and in business," said Ernie. "Even some internal competition is good for a company, as long as it's honest and promotes teamwork."

Ernie then allowed me the honor at the tenth tee. My drive had been coming on for the last couple of holes, so I stepped up with confidence and drove a beauty right down the middle. That left me with a nice wedge shot from about sixty-five yards.

"What do you think of that?" I asked Ernie, unable to wipe the grin from my face.

Without hesitation, Ernie stepped up to the tee and said, "OK, now I'll take *my* practice swing, and then we'll start the back nine."

Ernie always had a way of driving home a point. I enjoyed his company, his competitiveness, and most of the time, his humor. He was a very determined individual, and it crossed my mind that there was a good parallel between golf and leadership when it came to determination.

"You ever had one of those games where it seems for a stretch you've completely lost your swing?" I asked with anticipation.

"You bet," said Ernie, "makes me feel like a lumberjack instead of a golfer. But I've found that if you work your way through it, your swing does come back. And by the way, those stretches are often longer than for a few holes in a game. I've had them last for months. The swing isn't the only thing, either. There are plenty of low spots with putting, chipping, and just overall course management—you know, the decision-making part."

"Sounds like leadership to me," I chimed in.

"You're right on cue," said Ernie. "Leadership is not for the faint of heart. The low spots include working long hours to solve a problem, experiencing conflict with fellow employees, customers, and suppliers, suffering big egos, and having to meet unrealistic expectations. But the cream of the crop will push on, drive for results, and usually achieve more than expected."

We finished the 17th hole, and were all tied up. Ernie was now showing great signs of enthusiasm and a really positive attitude. It was contagious. We both hit great drives, and were then in position to birdie the last hole.

"So it comes down to the final putt," said Ernie. "I admire your enthusiasm, and that, too, is a sign of a great leader."

Ernie sank his putt for a birdie, and, being the gentleman that he can be when he wants to be, never said a word. He just let me putt. I missed that putt and Ernie won the game, but I really felt that we were both winners in the walk of life that day.

We decided to end our day with a pint in the clubhouse. As we were sipping our beer, Ernie told me of a time when he was sitting in the same clubhouse and overheard a conversation between two ladies who had just finished their round.

"One lady told the other that it was a great day for golf and they both agreed. Then the same lady said, 'I just got a brand new set of clubs for my husband.' The other lady thought for a moment, and then replied, 'Good trade!'"

"OK, Ernie," I said, "but remember that a man will blame anyone or anything for accidents he feels weren't his fault. But he feels personally responsible when he makes a hole-in-one!"

"Let's go home," said Ernie.

14

Most People Like Change

THE LAST COUPLE of months had been extremely hectic. There was so much change taking place with systems, new hires, a shuffle in the management team, and the acquisition of another company. All exciting stuff, but it had taken its toll on me and on many of my people. You could see the droopy eyes and lack of energy from too little sleep and too many crappy, late-night meals at the office. I thought I should let Ernie know that we needed a break.

"Ernie," I began, "all the change that's taking place right now is very rewarding to me, but I think my people need a bit of time off to re-charge their batteries. Do you think it's a good idea?"

"I've been many places and seen many things, most of which have experienced a tremendous amount of change. Therefore, I have considerable wisdom on this subject. To be blunt: of course you and your people should get recharged, assuming you won't miss any critical deadlines. But you just said that all this change is very rewarding. Do your people share the same sentiment?" asked Ernie.

"I *think* they do, but I've never really sought their input in that regard," I said a little sheepishly.

"Probably worth the effort—that's what leaders do," said Ernie. "Here's a question for you: Most people like change—true or false?"

"That's a no-brainer—the answer is 'false.' Most people do not like change, in fact, they resist it like hell," I said confidently.

"In the very many places I've been," started Ernie, "I have asked thousands of people this question. And you, my friend, are in the majority who thinks the answer is 'false.'"

"Doesn't surprise me," I said.

"What might surprise you," continued Ernie, "is that you and the majority are *wrong*. The correct answer is 'true.' Otherwise, how would you explain all the change we human beings always stir up, in order to make things better or to improve ourselves?"

"Makes sense," I responded, "but then why do so many people think the answer is 'false'?"

"Good question, and I have the answer. Listen carefully. It's not the change itself that people don't like, it's the *uncertainty* that goes along with the change. The fear of the unknown drives a lot of peculiar and resistant behavior, sometimes even from those responsible for initiating the change in the first place! When people see this behavior, they quickly conclude that people don't like change. *Not liking the change itself* versus *not liking the uncertainty around the change* is a critical distinction, especially if you want to be a leader and manage change well.

"If change is not managed well, the likely outcome is a return to the status quo. In other words, 'I'll be satisfied to be dissatisfied.' And when that happens, people either give up on the change or force it through using other fear tactics, and a lot of resources are wasted. If managed well, however, you can get past the uncertainty, and that leads to creativity and innovation *in addition to* the change. Once you begin to see things from a different perspective—a fearless perspective—all sorts of 'aha' moments occur and a sense of energy takes over. The good news is that this can be managed both at the personal level and the organizational level."

"How do you manage it?" I asked. This could really help me with the changes my people were going through.

"Before I answer your question directly, consider this well-known analogy," Ernie began. "Think back to the time when you were asked to take on your first supervisory position—and you had no background in leadership. In other words, you had no people skills. The apprehension could be overwhelming, but learning to supervise is like learning to ride a bike. Does a kid learn how to ride a bike the first time he tries? No, he gets on the bike, falls, gets up again, and keeps going until he learns how to ride. The key is, he *wants* to ride that bike. Supervising is no different. If you really want to do well at it, you stick with it, keep trying, and eventually you build self-confidence, your fears melt away, and you become good at it, as well. The best supervisors will have many 'aha' moments that lead to innovation, which turns them into leaders."

"So what are the specifics of 'change leadership,' since there is so much change going on all the time?" I asked. I wanted more than the bike riding comparison.

Ernie went to the whiteboard. "There are really four key things you need to do. How you do them is up to you, but here they are." On the whiteboard, he wrote the following:

1. **Start from within** — this comes from a strong self-belief and a positive attitude. For many leaders, this is the biggest change of all!
2. **Offer support** — people will follow your lead if they know you care about *them*.
3. **Walk your talk** — this old cliché is so important. People are more likely to try if they see you trying.
4. **Perseverance and passion** — it *is* like learning to ride a bike, and you have to love the journey.

After he finished writing and explaining each step, Ernie asked me, "So what kind of leader are you?"

Without hesitation I replied, "Well, I'm not a fast leader. And I'm not considered a slow leader, either. I guess that makes me a half-fast leader."

Ernie smiled and said, "You do need a break. Rest well."

15

Leadership vs. Management

IT OCCURRED TO me that many companies often miss the opportunity to tap into the creativity of their people. There always seem to be so many rules and policies that employees just blindly follow, because they think they are supposed to, or they are afraid, or they are just lazy. The reason doesn't really matter; the fact is, we are not taking advantage of a huge resource—which is free, in many ways—the minds of our people. This was something worth talking to Ernie about.

It was early on Saturday morning, and the weather was overcast and drizzly—the perfect day to sleep late. So I called Ernie on his cell phone. I figured if he had it switched on, he was either up, or he didn't mind being disturbed.

"Let's go to Tim Horton's," said Ernie, without even saying "hello" first. Caller ID has its advantages. "It's a perfect morning for a hot 'double-double' and a good chat with an old friend. I'll pick you up in ten minutes." Then he hung up. I would have to dress quickly, even if 'quickly' didn't want to be dressed....

Ernie arrived precisely ten minutes later. As I hopped into his truck he looked right at me and said, "I was hoping you would call this morning. In fact, I knew it was you as soon as my phone rang."

"Caller ID has a way of doing that," I said sarcastically.

"Actually, I didn't even look at my phone," said Ernie. "You're about the only person I know who would call my cell phone at 7:00 a.m. on a Saturday morning, so I just answered the phone."

"Oh," I said.

"Besides, even if it weren't you, it might have been someone who wanted to go for coffee, so I figured it was a low risk move," said Ernie.

"Is managing risk a leadership thing, or a management thing?" I asked, looking for an answer that might help me distinguish between management and leadership.

"Good question, but if you listen to your own words, the answer should be obvious," replied Ernie with a smile.

"Yeah, yeah," I fired back. "But really, people ask all the time what the difference is between management and leadership. How do *you* explain it?" I asked, hoping I would get Ernie's insight.

"I have asked the same question, over and over, of many people in many places. Therefore, I now possess the wisdom of the many, and have formulated, not just an opinion, but the actual, true answer," said Ernie in his most authoritative voice.

"I would really appreciate hearing the *actual, true* answer," I said.

"Let me borrow from a story you may remember from the Bible," began Ernie. "Now it seems that when Noah was informed of the weather forecast, he challenged everyone he could to begin building an ark. *That* would be called *leadership*. Once on the ark, Noah looked around and said, 'Make sure the elephants don't see what the rabbits are up to.' *That* would be called *management*."

I thought about that for a minute, funny as it was, and concluded that it wasn't a bad example to help understand the difference.

We stood in line at Timmy's for only a couple of minutes. This particular coffee shop had the process down pat, and made more revenue than most Tim Horton franchises in the country. Almost all the other shops in the franchise always had long lines of people who seemed glad to be waiting in them. It amazed me how people kept pouring in, but then the product *was* good, so the place has become a mecca for coffee lovers. It occurred to me that this particular Tim Hortons, with its high volume but shorter lines, could be an example of both leadership *and* management.

We sat down and enjoyed a few sips of hot coffee, while people-watching for awhile. It was actually quite entertaining—this location brought in all walks of life, and the people mixed quite well. They seemed genuinely happy, even though many came in dripping wet from the rain.

Finally, I broke the silence and said, "Ernie, you know full well that this Timmy's never seems to have a long line, compared to many others we have frequented. I have been watching the staff, and they really seem to have the processes down pat—they never even waste one second to say, 'Next, please.'"

"Good observation," said Ernie.

"So figuring out the processes would be a management thing, correct?" I asked.

"You bet," replied Ernie, "but it likely includes leadership as well. Watch the staff for a little longer and tell me what you see."

We watched for a little longer. This time I focused on how the staff interacted, both with each other and with the customers. The greetings were happy and genuine—you could tell by the smiles and the eye contact—and the customers smiled back. The staff were courteous to each other, too. Everyone pitched in and helped—the place was busy and no one was ever idle. Even the busboys (and busgirls) were polite and did not drag their feet at all.

"So what do you see?" asked Ernie.

"I see a lot of happy people, with genuine concern to get the job done," I replied, just thinking out loud.

"I see the same thing," said Ernie. "So let's suppose for a minute that the processes weren't quite as good as they seem to be. With the approach that these people take to working with each other, do you think they could still be as effective?"

"I think so," I said, a little cautiously. "I guess you mean that with good leadership, people will be happy and the processes don't matter as much?"

"You sound hesitant," said Ernie.

"Well, there has to be some point at which inefficient processes just become frustrating and burdensome. At that point, I think people will not be as happy and may even take out their frustrations on each other," I said.

"Good point!" Ernie jumped in. "Having a focus on people and the vision to see where you want to take them—that's leadership. Managing day-to-day operations, improving processes, and getting the job done—that's management. That's why there is always this confusion over what's leadership, and what's management. In other words, it seems to me, the same people often do both, and I don't believe they stop to think, 'Hey, is this a management activity, or a leadership activity?' They just go about making decisions and doing what's best."

"That in itself could be considered leadership," I chimed in.

Without hesitation, Ernie continued, "Now I think you're getting it. At the same time, remember that some people are very capable of wearing both hats, and some aren't. I would argue that everyone has a role in leadership, that it's not just reserved for the top echelon. However, if the top echelon is not leading, their people will soon become frustrated and not do their jobs in the best way possible, or even leave the company."

"So," I began, "if we get back to our discussion about this coffee shop, the owners and managers must create a good atmosphere to keep the staff happy, as well as institute the processes that will be the most efficient."

"Perfect conclusion," said Ernie. "And to take it one step further, with the right leadership, everybody contributes ideas for improving processes. We all know that the people doing it will have the best ideas for changes, in order to make their own lives easier. But they have to feel comfortable speaking up. That's where leadership comes in."

"I get the picture, but one more thing: I think there are plenty of examples where a person can be very good at managing, but not leading, and vice-versa. Do you agree?" I asked.

"I have been to many Timmy's, and have drunk many 'double-doubles,' which put me in a position of perfect authority. The answer is: most definitely," Ernie said with conviction. "And the companies that recognize this make sure they put the right people in the right jobs. This takes considerable foresight, thought, strategy, and, of course—leadership.

"One more coffee, then let's go smell the rain."

16

Heavy Thinking

IT WAS MONDAY morning, and I had been up later than usual the night before. I wasn't tired, but I certainly had a lot of things on my mind. I had been struggling with one of my direct reports—we just couldn't seem to get on the same wavelength. But I believed she had a ton of potential, both in her current role as a manager, and in her future roles with the company in a more senior capacity.

So I drove to work even earlier than I normally do. I knew I would find Ernie laying out his plans for the week. When I arrived, he was having a coffee and seemed to be in a good mood.

"Ernie," I started, wanting to get right to the point.

"I've been many places and seen many things. As a result, I have been called many things: 'Ernie' is just fine, but 'good morning' would seem to be more appropriate on such a grand day," Ernie said.

This stopped me in my tracks, because I knew he was right. I was so eager to get to my own dilemma that I didn't even give him a proper greeting.

"Good morning, Ernie," I said sincerely.

"That's more like it," said Ernie. "But I do sense you have something on your mind. Take a seat and let's talk."

"Thank you." I sat down and got comfortable. "Last night I was doing some heavy thinking."

Ernie looked me right in the eye and said, "You did say *thinking*, did you not?"

"Gotcha," I said. "Maybe I should have done something else even heavier, but thinking is what I did." I then paused for a moment, because I knew from experience that Ernie would rarely let me get right to the point. It was his way of slowing down and thinking things through a little better. And it usually worked.

Then Ernie went off on a short tangent, which actually gave me something else to think about. "In my travels, I once met a gentleman who had become a real thinker, and it was completely intentional. He would plan when to think, and what to think about. It only became a problem when he started to think at work. Personally, I believe this is most unfortunate. People should be encouraged to think at work—it leads to much more creativity. But I find that most companies discourage it, and this fellow's organization was no exception.

"He told me that one day his boss called him in and said, 'Listen, I value you as an employee, so this is difficult for me to say. But you've developed a real thinking problem, and everybody knows about it. If I let it go, others may follow and start thinking as well. I must demand that you stop thinking on the job, or look for employment elsewhere.'

"I asked this fellow what he did. He told me he had no choice—the union rules prevented thinking on the job. Only the union leaders were allowed to think and dream up new rules."

I thought about this for a minute. "OK, you got me. Is this a true story?"

"Actually, it is. I've embellished it a little, so it's like the movies they make today—you know, 'based on a true story'? The point is, thinking *is* important. I'm not talking about daydreaming all day long, but actually scheduling some 'think-time' and not just being haphazard about it. Some people have challenged me on this by saying, 'Ernie, I do lots of thinking, especially when I'm driving.' The problem is, they are not being systematic about it."

"So how do you make it work?" I asked, now realizing we were off topic from what I came there for, but nevertheless, I was interested.

"Good question," said Ernie. "So here's what you do. And keep in mind, these are specific steps to get the most out of scheduled 'think-time.' In no way does it replace your ongoing thinking, like the driving example. Random thoughts are good. But to solve problems or find new opportunities, try this." At this point Ernie walked over to his whiteboard and wrote the following:

1. Schedule "think-time" on your calendar—three times a week for fifteen minutes at a time.
2. While you are "thinking," take out a notepad and jot down your thoughts using mind-maps. These help with creativity.
3. Be aware of what pops into your mind when you are doing other things that don't require thinking.

"So what you are saying," I interjected, "is that you don't actually have to solve the problem or figure out the opportunity in a single 'think-time' setting. The ideas and answers will pop into your head when your mind is less cluttered."

"You got it. Now go and try it," said Ernie.

I left, confident that I could solve the problem with my manager with a little "think-time."

17

What Do You Look for in a Leader?

"HEY!" I SHOUTED, catching Ernie by surprise as he headed into the men's room.

"Hay," Ernie said with a pause, "is for horses, so the saying goes. But it's really the alfalfa they are after. And besides, right now I have to 'riss like a pace horse,' alfalfa or not, so I have no time for idle chatter."

"It can wait," I responded. I really wasn't in a hurry. I had been thinking about something I wanted to ask Ernie, and just happened to run into him in the hallway. I should have known he was preoccupied, just judging by the strides he was taking towards the men's room.

"No, it can't," and off he went, so to speak.

Wiping his hands dry on a paper towel, he returned with a smile on his face. He walked up to me and confidently extended his hand in a handshake. I reached out to reciprocate, although not with the same sense of confidence.

"Today is a great day," said Ernie. "I know they all are, but this one is particularly great."

I thought it would be my turn to speak, especially after waiting for him to go to the men's room. Nevertheless, I gave in and asked the obvious, "What makes it so great?"

"We just hired a new person, and I think she is going to be a great leader for us," pronounced Ernie.

I couldn't believe it: I had come looking for Ernie to reinforce some ideas I had about what makes a great leader. And here he was saying he had just hired one! If I could tap into his thinking as to why he hired her in the first place, I would have my answer. But I didn't want him to know that he had—rudely, I thought—anticipated what I was going to talk to him about, so I asked in a nonchalant way, "So tell me, what do you actually look for in a leader?"

Ernie thought carefully before replying. Finally, he said, "Let's go to Timmy's and grab a coffee. This deserves a good chat."

So off we went. Our timing was good as the line wasn't too long, and we were quickly sitting down, each with a fresh cup of coffee.

"In my travels, I met a young lady by the name of Cyndi, who imparted to me great knowledge that has added to my wisdom. Based on what she told me, I think it's important to partially answer your question by talking about what you *don't* look for in a leader. Don't forget, I've been many places and seen many things. Part of this experience is with good

leaders and bad leaders. So, I have gained much knowledge about both," Ernie said.

"How could I forget?" I muttered. "Anyway, what do you *not* look for?"

"When I am trying to find a good leader, I think it is paramount to not look for someone who is just like me," Ernie stated.

"No one else on Earth could have that much wisdom," I said caustically.

"Very funny," chortled Ernie. "But seriously, it is a common mistake. Many people make a quick connection with other folks who are similar to them in personality, work style, or attitudes. When building a leadership team, you need diversity. I wouldn't rule out someone who is like me, as long as I believe he or she can adapt to changing situations. I just mean to be careful not to base such a big decision solely on connecting with like personalities."

"Makes sense," I said, "so what else is important?"

"It is important not to judge a book by its cover. By this I mean physical appearance, background, and personal beliefs. As long as someone's personal values are in line with the company's, there shouldn't be a problem," replied Ernie.

"An example—?" I started to ask.

"An example would be," Ernie snapped back, "the introvert who personally values having a couple of close friends, contrasted with the extrovert who needs to be around lots of people most of the time. Both the introvert and the extrovert can align themselves with a corporate value that supports strong working relationships and teamwork. However, in another example, if someone wanted to contribute to a company simply by showing up and getting the job done, but the company puts a strong value on learning and change, there is likely to be a misalignment. It doesn't make the individual a bad person, just not a good fit for that company."

At this point I started taking a few notes. I had a hunch they would come in handy later on. "Ernie, I know it's a pretty deep subject, and there is no magic formula for finding the best leaders, but can you give me an idea of some of the things that stand out in your mind when you are looking for leaders?"

"You're right," said Ernie, "there is no magic formula, but there are some traits that I think are critically important. In my travels I once met a real estate investment guru who was very motivational. He suggested that we all need to be leaders in our own right and that the most important ingredient in a leader is credibility."

"Incredible!" I threw that in for kicks.

"Actually, it is," continued Ernie, not missing a beat. "All too often, I hear people talk about the importance of building credibility in order to be successful in business and even in life. Yet this guy was the first person I ever heard explain *how* you build and maintain credibility with the people in your life."

"You've got my attention," I said, pencil and paper ready.

"There are five things you need to do to establish and maintain credibility," Ernie stated. "To set the record straight, this real estate guru told us the first four, and the fifth was added by a colleague of mine when we were teaching a group of salespeople one year.

"The advice may appear simple when you first hear it, but think about each step carefully, and I'm sure you will find it as profound as I did. These are not in priority order, so the first one I'll give you is this: 'Show up on time.'"

I wrote it down and then asked the obvious, "Isn't that a no-brainer?"

"To people like you, who practice it all the time, it goes without saying; it's part of your belief system. The key to it all, and this goes for all five points, is the word *consistently*.

Think about someone you know who is always late. You know, the type who you tell the meeting starts at 8:45 a.m. when it really starts at 9:00 a.m.?"

"I can think of a few, and not just at work," I replied.

"Now think of someone you know who is always on time, not just for meetings, but for everything they do," said Ernie.

"My father was that way," I replied. "You could set your watch by him, but then you would realize that your watch was now five minutes fast."

"So who has more credibility? You see where I'm going with this. It's simple advice, but it's so important if you want to have credibility.

"The second point is: 'Finish what you start.' Too many people start lots of things, little projects, you name it, and rarely finish most of them.

"The third point is: 'Do what you say you're going to do.' Again, how many times have you been in meetings where people commit to action plans, and then nothing happens? A true leader is one who follows through." Ernie seemed to be on a roll now.

I interrupted, "Hold on, the second and third points seem awfully similar."

"Yes, they do," said Ernie, "and they actually are related. However, there are times when finishing what you start is not based on a commitment you made to anyone other than yourself. So it is worth the distinction."

"Carry on," I begged, still taking copious notes.

"The fourth point is: 'Say "please" and "thank you."' Now this is something you should have learned at your mother's knee, but think about how many people don't follow that advice. It's common courtesy and goes a long way to making people feel appreciated. Again, the key is consistency, and in this case I would add, sincerity."

"And the fifth, please?" I asked. Sincerely.

"The fifth point is: 'Always tell the truth.' Again, it sounds like a no-brainer: who would want to have a liar for a leader? But if you dig deep enough into all the information that is communicated in companies, families, the media, you name it—there seem to be a lot of 'half-truths' out there. Do you agree?" asked Ernie.

"I'd be lying if I didn't," I quickly replied. "Seems to me I recall a quote by Mark Twain that goes something like, 'If you always tell the truth, then you don't have to remember anything.'"

"Good advice," said Ernie. "So, do you have the five points?"

"I sure do," I replied. I showed Ernie my note pad, which had a quick summary of the five points:

1. Show up on time.
2. Finish what you start.
3. Do what you say you're going to do.
4. Say "please" and "thank you."
5. Always tell the truth.

Note: Be *consistent* with all five!

After Ernie nodded his approval at the fact that I could actually take notes, I asked him, "So how do you know whether a person has these traits?"

"Good question," Ernie said. "Everyone will *say* they do all five, even if you try to find a clever way to ask about it in an interview. The proof is always in people's behaviors over time. But you *can* ask good questions to get at the crux of each point, and then, be prepared to listen carefully to what they are saying 'between the lines,' so to speak. For starters, did they show up for the interview on time? Did they come prepared based on previous discussions? Of course, if it is an internal candidate, you should have had lots of opportunities to observe these behaviors."

I had much to think about, especially this: if I were to look in the mirror with a critical eye, could I be honest and say that I was *consistent-*

ly doing all five? If not, I would have to create an immediate action plan to close the gaps.

"I've been thinking of adding a sixth point," said Ernie.

This caught me by surprise, so I took out my pencil and paper again.

"People often give the word 'ego' a bad rap, as if you are a bad person if you have a big ego. This is unfortunate, because the fact is, everyone has an ego: it's just how it's perceived by others that can be a problem. My belief is that having a big ego is good, *if* it can help boost your confidence and self-esteem. However, if it gets so big that decisions are made based on self-interest, then that actually denotes a lack of confidence, and that is not good for any leader.

"But the nice thing about egotists is that they don't talk about other people."

I took my last gulp of coffee, and walked back to the office with Ernie. In silence.

18

Letters to Ernie

Dear Ernie:

Our company keeps talking about "best practices." What is your opinion on this approach?

***Dear Best*:**

It is my much valued opinion that "best practices" tend to emerge when there is a severe loss, like in sports.

Dear Ernie:

I always try to follow the Golden Rule when dealing with other people. Do you believe in this philosophy?

***Dear Goldie*:**

First of all, what I believe in is not important, nor is a philosophy important. It's what you do *that counts. So I don't look at the Golden Rule as a philosophy, but rather as a guide for my behavior; I learned this from my mother. But I don't follow it anyway, and still my mother has forgiven me. I try to behave according to the Platinum Rule—treat others the way they want to be treated, unless they are asking for unearned money or are engaging in unethical behavior.*

Dear Ernie:

My boss has demanded that I set some goals for the year. I've done this many times over my career, and quite honestly it seems like a waste of time, when all people do is write down what

the boss wants to hear. How should I respond to these demands?

Dear Goalie:

Tell him your intentions. *He may still want to call them "goals," but who cares what you call them? Think hard about what you* intend *to do this year—you'll find this a much more powerful way to articulate what you* will *do. If you have teenage daughters, you'll know what I mean. I don't ask the boys they bring by what their goals are, I ask them their intentions. How they struggle with the answer gives me a lot more insight into what their actions are going to be.*

Dear Ernie:

I think one of my employees is insane. I want to be a good leader, so what should I do?

Dear Insane:

Personally, I don't suffer from insanity. I enjoy every minute of it.

Dear Ernie:

I took a management course and they went on and on about decision making. They even introduced a model that is supposed to help you make a decision. I think I spend more time using the model than I do implementing my decisions. Now I can't decide whether or not to keep using the model!

***Dear Decider*:**

I, too, used to be indecisive. Now I'm not sure....

Dear Ernie:

I used to work in fear everyday. I always thought my employees were after my job, and I often closed my office door, thinking it would prevent my boss from chewing me out. Then I met some people who helped me immensely. Do you think your readers would be interested in how I overcame this?

***Dear Fearful*:**

You'd have to ask them. And you need to understand that just because you are no longer paranoid, does not mean that people aren't out to get you.

Dear Ernie:

I am constantly being badgered by employees who say they want a piece of the action;

you know, they want some kind of ownership in the business. My concern is that they are employees for a reason. Can they really handle the entrepreneurial skills that go along with ownership?

Dear Offtrepreneur:
Keep in mind that the owner of a home is always just coming out of a hardware store. And a lot of homeowners enjoy that—if they don't, they are better off being renters. I think it is the same with companies—some employees will do what it takes to be an owner, others are better off just renting the space. And companies need both of those kinds of people.

Dear Ernie:
How important is experience when you are looking to hire someone?

Dear Experience:
Good judgment comes from experience. And experience, well, that comes from bad judgment. Who would you hire?

Dear Ernie:

Many people talk about the importance of values and principles when it comes to leading a company. Do you have principles that you lead by?

Dear Valued:

Of course I do. And if you don't like them, I have others.

Dear Ernie:

I have been looking at how our company is structured, which is by function. I am wondering if this is the best structure, given that each function seems to have an entirely different way of thinking. Do you share this view?

Dear Structured:

I don't share it often. But I do agree, each function has its own way of thinking. A good leader will set up teams that take advantage of this diversity, but it needs to be managed well. Here is a sample of how these different functions think:

Engineering: "How will this work?"
IT: "Why will this work?"
Management: "When will this work?"
Sales: "Do you want fries with that?"

Thank You

ONE SUNNY DAY several months ago, my good friend, Ches Beerling, met me for a round of golf in beautiful British Columbia. Not too long into the round, I hit an errant fairway shot and Ches immediately said, “I’ve been many places and seen many things, but I’ve never seen a golf shot like that!” I laughed like crazy, but got a little choked up at the same time. Ches had read my late father’s book, *The Travels of Ernie*, and it was obvious that the infamous line had made an impact.

I realized that I indeed had travelled many places myself and met many interesting people in my quest to gather some of the best leadership stories ever. I am grateful to all these people for their contributions to my stories. In some cases, I deliberately picked people’s brains to understand how their leadership experiences had made an impact on them. In other cases, I was inspired by the actions of certain people or by the conversations we had. Each lesson is based on a true story, with the names changed (to protect the innocent!). There are two exceptions to this, because, in those stories, I wanted to do justice to the brave individuals involved: the incredible feat of Jack McBride recounted in

"Teamwork is Dangerous," and the inspiring story of Billy Drew and his kindhearted friend, Ches Beerling, retold in "Walk a Mile in My Shoes."

The end result is some life lessons that I truly hope will take us all to the next level. I have many other people to thank for either their direct or indirect input to my stories: Jim Beddow, David Sandmeyer, Pat Ryan, Walt Stevenson, Gary Ritland, Jim Brown, Matt Kenna, Blane Charles, Scott Morris, Ray Mills, Keith Lumby, Barry Davis, Ron Campbell, Dr. Paul Hersey, Scott Knutson, Shawn Morton, Justin Moss, Jennifer Smith, Lois Mitchell, Gord Piper, Ron Montgomery, Robert Mills, Mick Mercurio, Wes Jacobson, Paul Cahill, Peter Van Maarion, Tim O'Connor, Merlynn Mantik, Tim Johnson, Dan Stamp, John West, Bill Forrest, Lyle Kehoe, Duane Brownlee, David Place, Todd Schmick, John White, Andrew Sherwood, Colin Sauer, Don Murray, Kurt Goodjohn, Bill Forrest, Brock Brown and Brian Parsley.

Of course, I could not have done this without the support of my family, many of whom contributed to the stories as well: my lovely daughters, Cyndi and Sarah; my ever creative son, Dale; my first-class sister, Brenda McKenney; and my supportive brothers, Dennis and Dan. My mother, Ellen, is the "rock" behind us all, and her encouragement is unsurpassed.

When I first met Jeffrey Gitomer in 2004 (who now has ten best-selling books on the market), I told him I wanted to write a book. His quick response was, "You *gotta* write a book!" Jeffrey has inspired many people to write, and that day certainly put me on the path. A while ago I was bouncing ideas off all kinds of experts and friends to come up with the best title for this book. Then I met up with Jeffrey when he was speaking in Calgary, and he penned the title on a yellow sticky note, which I will keep forever. Jeffrey, I thank you so much for your generosity, your inspiration, and your endless creativity.

Credit should also go to Solomon Asch and Milton Rokeach for their extensive research into human psychology, which I was able to access over the Internet.

A special thanks goes to Rick Menard for all the illustrations in this book, including the cover. And last, but in no way least, a special thanks to Gabriella Deponte for her patient editing, which has made such a wonderful difference to the final product.

About the Author

Murray Robert Janewski grew up in Calgary, Alberta, Canada, the most beautiful city in the foothills of the Rocky Mountains. He had a fun-filled childhood with sports, family camping, and music, which set the stage for the variety of passions he carries with him to this day.

After a long and varied career in the oil and gas industry, Murray started ACT One International Corporation (www.aoic.ca). ACT One is a training and consulting company that focuses on helping growing companies in leadership, sales, and customer service.

Murray now lives in Calgary, Alberta, and has three grown children: Cyndi, Dale, and Sarah. They get together as often as they can to enjoy the love of family and, of course, to share a laugh or two.

Printed in the United States
By Bookmasters